Happy 4TH OF JULY

ABBIE MERCER

PowerKiDS press™

New York

For Michelle

Published in 2008 by The Rosen Publishing Group, Inc.
29 East 21st Street, New York, NY 10010

First Edition

Editor: Amelie von Zumbusch
Book Design: Julio Gil
Photo Researcher: Nicole Pristash

Photo Credits: Cover, pp. 1, 5, 9, 11, 13, 13 (inset), 15, 17, 19, 19 (inset), 21 © Shutterstock.com; p. 7 © Getty Images.

Library of Congress Cataloging-in-Publication Data

Mercer, Abbie.
   Happy 4th of July / Abbie Mercer. — 1st ed.
      p. cm. — (Holiday fun)
   Includes index.
   ISBN-13: 978-1-4042-3810-7 (library binding)
   ISBN-10: 1-4042-3810-7 (library binding)
   1. Fourth of July—Juvenile literature. 2. Fourth of July celebrations—Juvenile literature. I. Title.
   E286.A1394 2008
   394.2634—dc22
                                                2007002572

Manufactured in the United States of America.

Contents

Independence Day — 4

A British Colony — 6

The Declaration of Independence — 8

Red, White, and Blue! — 10

How to Make an American Flag — 12

Parades — 14

Picnics and Barbecues — 16

How to Make a Red, White, and Blue Desert — 18

Fireworks — 20

Happy 4th of July! — 22

Glossary — 23

Index — 24

Web Sites — 24

Independence Day

Every July 4, Americans **celebrate** a holiday that honors their country. We call this holiday the 4th of July, after the day on which it is celebrated. It is also called **Independence** Day. This is because the United States claimed its independence from England on July 4, 1776.

On Independence Day, Americans honor their country's history and values. They put up American **flags**, sing **patriotic** songs, march in parades, and put on fireworks shows. The 4th of July is a time to remember the people who fought for our freedom and to think about how to make the United States a better country.

This boy is proudly carrying an American flag in honor of the 4th of July.

A British Colony

In the 1600s and 1700s, the land that would become the United States was 13 British colonies. Colonies are places where people settle that are still ruled by the country from which those people came.

Over time, the American colonists came to think it was unfair for them to be ruled by the king of faraway England. They were angry that they had no say in setting up the laws they followed and the taxes they paid. The colonists grew even angrier after the British started taking away many of their rights. In 1775, war broke out between them.

The war the American colonists fought with the British is known as the American Revolution.

The Declaration of Independence

When war broke out, the colonists were not sure they wanted to break away from England for good. They decided to meet in Philadelphia, Pennsylvania, to consider what to do. Each of the 13 colonies sent people to talk over this question.

After much thought, the colonists decided to break with England. Thomas Jefferson, a colonist from Virginia, wrote a **Declaration** of Independence, which explained why the Americans were doing this. In it, he wrote that the Americans believed that "all men are created equal" and that people have "**unalienable** Rights," such as "Life, Liberty and the **pursuit** of Happiness."

The colonists adopted the Declaration of Independence on July 4, 1776, at Philadelphia's Independence Hall.

Red, White, and Blue!

After breaking away from England, the Americans decided to make their own flag. The first American flag had a blue square in the top left corner with a circle of 13 white stars in it. The flag also had 13 red or white stripes.

The 13 stars and stripes stood for the colonies of New Hampshire, Massachusetts, Connecticut, Rhode Island, New York, New Jersey, Pennsylvania, Delaware, Maryland, Virginia, North Carolina, South Carolina, and Georgia. After the American Revolution, these colonies became states. As the country added more states, the flag got more stars. Today the flag has 50 stars.

Many people celebrate the 4th of July by wearing the colors of the American flag.

How to Make an American Flag

Lots of people hang up American flags to celebrate the 4th of July. Here is how you can make your own American flag.

1

Start your flag with a piece of paper that is 11 inches (28 cm) long by 6 inches (15 cm) wide.

2

Find a piece of red paper the same length as the white paper. Cut four bands that are ½ inch (1.3 cm) wide and 11 inches (28 cm) long out of the paper. Then cut three strips that are ½ inch (1.3 cm) wide and 11 inches (28 cm) long. Glue the bands to the white paper. Space the bands evenly and let the top and bottom ones go a bit over the sides of the white paper.

3

Cut a rectangle out of blue paper that is 4½ inches (11.5 cm) by 3½ inches (9 cm). Glue it to the top left corner of the flag. Line it up with the red stripes.

4

Make 50 small stars that are each ½ inch (1.3 cm) across. Look carefully at the flag on page 13, and glue the stars to the flag. If you have star stickers, you could use them instead of cutting out the stars.

Things That You Will Need

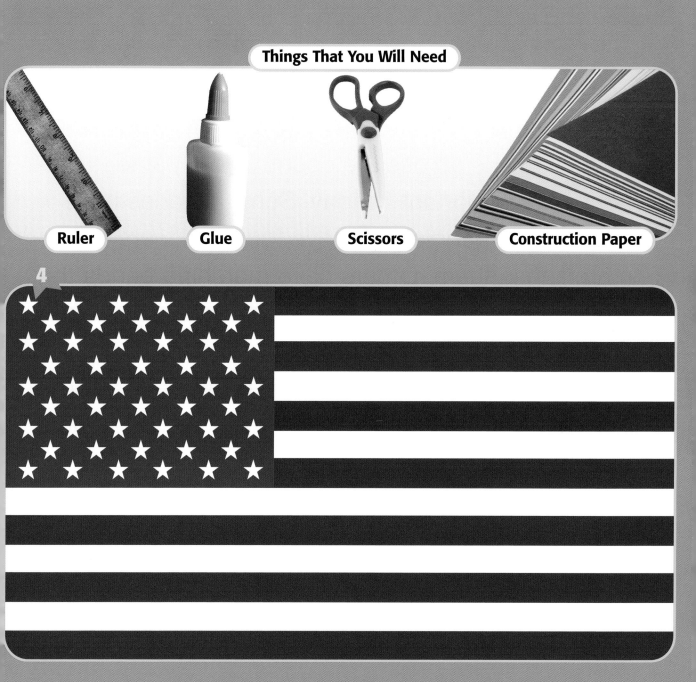

Ruler

Glue

Scissors

Construction Paper

4

Parades

Parades are another way people celebrate the 4th of July. Towns across the country hold parades to honor this important holiday. Some parades have veterans, or people who have fought in wars, marching in them. Others have marching bands that play patriotic music.

One of the biggest parades takes place in the country's capital, Washington, D.C. Marching bands from all over the country march in the parade. More than 300,000 people watch the parade each year. Provo, Utah, holds a big parade as part of its America's Freedom Festival celebration. The parade has horses, music, dancers, and big balloons.

This veteran is driving a patriotic car in a 4th of July parade.

Picnics and Barbecues

Many people celebrate the 4th of July by meeting up with friends and family to have a feast. Since the 4th of July falls in the middle of the summer, people often decide to eat outside. A meal that you eat outside is called a picnic. People eat cold foods like sandwiches, chips, and fruit at their 4th of July picnics. They spread cloths out on the grass and enjoy the beautiful outdoors as they eat.

People also hold **barbecues** outside for the 4th of July. At barbecues, people eat foods such as hot dogs, hamburgers, and barbecued chicken.

People often make kebabs, which are pieces of meat or vegetables cooked on a stick, at 4th of July barbecues.

How to Make a Red, White, and Blue Desert

You can use whipped cream, blueberries, and strawberries to make a desert with the colors of the American flag to eat at your picnic or barbecue.

1
Put 2 cups (473 ml) of heavy cream into a big bowl.

2
Use the high setting of an electric mixer to whip, or beat, the cream. The cream is ready when it plops, instead of pours, out of a spoon.

3
Mix 4 tablespoons (22.5 g) powdered sugar into the whipped cream, like the people on page 19. If the whipped cream seems too thick, you can add a tiny bit of unwhipped cream to make it softer.

4
Wash some blueberries and strawberries. Cut the tops off the strawberries and cut them in half. Put the fruit into bowls with the whipped cream, as seen on page 19.

Fireworks

Fireworks are another big part of most people's 4th of July celebrations. After they have finished eating their picnics or barbecued food, many people set off to watch a fireworks show. Some people even decide to have their picnics near the spot where the fireworks will be held.

One of the best-known 4th of July fireworks shows takes place in Boston, Massachusetts. Every year more than 400,000 people gather along the city's Charles River to watch thousands of fireworks go off. Well-known bands and the Boston Pops **Orchestra** supply music to go along with the fireworks.

Fireworks come in many different colors, shapes, and sizes.

Happy 4th of July!

Fireworks, picnics, parades, and barbecues are only a few of the many fun **traditions** tied to the 4th of July. Lots of people play or watch baseball games on the 4th of July. Eating contests are another common 4th of July tradition. In an eating contest, many people all try to see who can eat the most food. Common foods for eating contests are hot dogs or pies.

Some towns and cities hold public readings of the Declaration of Independence. This lets people remember our country's history and think about the important ideas on which our country is based.

Glossary

barbecues (BAHR-bih-kyooz) Meals cooked outside on a grill or over an open fire.

celebrate (SEH-luh-brayt) To honor an important moment by doing special things.

declaration (deh-kluh-RAY-shun) An official statement of something.

flags (FLAGZ) Pieces of cloth that stand for a country or group.

independence (in-duh-PEN-dents) Freedom from the control of other people.

orchestra (OR-kes-truh) A group of people who play music together.

patriotic (pay-tree-AH-tik) Showing love for one's country.

pursuit (pur-SOOT) The act of trying to get or to seek something.

traditions (truh-DIH-shunz) Ways of doing something that have been passed down over time.

unalienable (un-AYL-yeh-neh-bul) Cannot be given or taken away.

Index

A

Americans, 4, 8, 10

B

barbecue(s), 16, 18

C

colonies, 6, 8, 10
colonist(s), 6, 8

D

Declaration of
    Independence, 8, 22

E

England, 4, 6, 8, 10

F

flag(s), 4, 10, 12, 18

H

history, 4, 22

P

parades, 4, 14, 22
Philadelphia,
    Pennsylvania, 8

R

rights, 6, 8

T

taxes, 6
thought, 8
traditions, 22

U

United States, 4, 6

V

Virginia, 8, 10

Web Sites

Due to the changing nature of Internet links, PowerKids Press has developed an online list of Web sites related to the subject of this book. This site is updated regularly. Please use this link to access the list:
www.powerkidslinks.com/fun/july/